AIR WAR COLLEGE

AIR UNIVERSITY

BOMBER REQUIREMENTS:

FROM THE TOP-DOWN

by

Samuel C. Seager, Lt. Col., USAF

A Research Report Submitted to the Faculty

In Partial Fulfillment of the Graduation Requirements

Advisor: Col. Richard L. Hamer

Maxwell Air Force Base, Alabama

April 1998

Report Documentation Page

Report Date	Report Type	Dates Covered (from... to)
01APR1998	N/A	-

Title and Subtitle	Contract Number
Bomber Requirements: From the Top-Down	Grant Number
	Program Element Number

Author(s)	Project Number
Seager, Samuel C.	Task Number
	Work Unit Number

Performing Organization Name(s) and Address(es)	Performing Organization Report Number
Air War College Maxwell AFB, Al 36112	

Sponsoring/Monitoring Agency Name(s) and Address(es)	Sponsor/Monitor's Acronym(s)
	Sponsor/Monitor's Report Number(s)

Distribution/Availability Statement
Approved for public release, distribution unlimited

Supplementary Notes
The original document contains color images.

Abstract

Subject Terms

Report Classification	Classification of this page
unclassified	unclassified

Classification of Abstract	Limitation of Abstract
unclassified	UU

Number of Pages
79

Disclaimer

The views expressed in this academic research paper are those of the author(s) and do not reflect the official policy or position of the US government or the Department of Defense. In accordance with Air Force Instruction 51-303, it is not copyrighted, but is the property of the United States government.

Contents

Illustrations

Tables

Preface

The US bomber force faces a significant modernization challenge. As the weapon of choice for rapidly projecting national resolve over intercontinental distances, the bomber force must prepare for the future by establishing a wide array of capabilities across the entire spectrum of conflict. However, our current modernization process is bogged down in a short-view, threat-based planning cycle. Instead, bomber modernization must come to grips with a wide range of requirements addressing future conflict. These essential requirements which stem from a series of military studies and vision documents place a premium on flexibility in operations. The bomber force must begin now to expand its modernization effort toward flexible avionics, weaponry, logistics, and training if it hopes to compete as a viable tool in future conflict.

This project is based on my strong belief in the efficacy of airpower and the utility of long-range strike aviation in serving national interests, however, it is not a solo effort. I need to acknowledge the staff and faculty of the Air War College for expanding my limited vision of future conflict. In particular, I want to thank my advisor, Col Richard Hamer for his insight, patience, and the hours spent pouring over drafts. Likewise, I must thank Dr. Jim Mowbray for his masterful work in the arena of airpower theory, strategy, and doctrine and Dr. Mike Hickok for forcing me to think beyond the operational arena. Finally, and above all, thanks to Cindy, Dacey, Payton, and Kallie for their understanding and support over the many hours involved in completing this project.

Abstract

This research effort defines bomber force requirements with one eye on national security and military strategy and the other on the future. It attempts to bridge our leadership's void in defining future roles and requirements for the nation's bomber force. Targeted for developers of requirements at Headquarters Air Force and Air Combat Command, this paper distills the lessons of historical bomber operations as well as guidance contained in documents ranging from the National Security Strategy through Air Force Basic Doctrine to define the current roles and capabilities demanded of bombers. The paper then tackles the nature of future conflict and the unique missions and capabilities required by that operating environment. As a capstone, the paper then delineates specific requirements in terms of avionics, weaponry, logistics, and training. This synthesis of requirements forms a modernization roadmap ensuring the responsiveness and viability of the US bomber force in supporting military strategy across the spectrum of future conflict.

Chapter 1

Introduction

Our nation's bomber force is in peril -- its enemies: a lack of vision concerning requirements, overwhelming inertia behind outdated support concepts, and a siege mentality in aircrew training. These problems are certainly not insurmountable, but if not addressed they will be the death knells of our bomber fleet. I will attack these problems, not from a parochial perspective but from the standpoint of determining the essential capabilities required to effectively employ bombers in support of national objectives. In this paper I provide a methodical analysis of the past, current, and future roles of bombers then translate these missions into an overarching set of requirements. More specifically, I begin by outlining bomber missions within the historical context of selected air campaigns and operations since World War II. Next, by sifting through strategy and doctrine publications, I examine current bomber roles. Then, getting to the heart of the matter, I explore several studies and "vision" documents to provide insight concerning future bomber missions. Finally, I translate these missions into a broad set of requirements focusing on avionics, weaponry, support concepts, and training. The desired end state is to provide a coherent plan for the evolution of US bomber forces. However, before defining these requirements I must first answer one key question, "Does this nation need bombers at all?"

Chapter 2

A Case for Bombers

Cutting right to the heart of this question, detractors often argue that land- and carrier-based fighter aircraft can easily absorb the roles performed by bombers; there's no longer a need to bear the expense of maintaining bomber forces. To a degree, they're correct. In terms of one weapon over one target, it matters little what type of airframe delivers that weapon as long as the desired effect is achieved. However, operational concerns dictate wider considerations. Chief among these is the principle of mass.

Mass

Mass, or the amount of firepower over a target, provides lethal leverage against target sets. Despite the emphasis the Air Force currently places on the lethality of expensive precision guided munitions (PGMs), many target sets exist which encompass broad areas consisting of numerous individual aim points. Classic examples of such "area targets" include rail marshalling yards, oil refining and storage facilities, armies in road march, and deployed arrays of ground forces.[1] Rather than targeting each aim point with expensive PGMs, bombers can saturate these area targets with relatively inexpensive general purpose munitions using a fraction of the force structure required to accomplish the same task with other air assets. For example, from Table 1, two B-52Hs can carry the same number of Mk-84 2,000lb. bombs as nine F-16s. Likewise, it requires seven F-16s to carry the same load of Mk-82 500lb. weapons as a single B-1B. Thus, the bombers' tremendous carriage, in effect, equates to massing forces over a target. Bombers hold this same comparative mass advantage in terms of guided weapons as well.

Table 1. Comparative Maximum Weapons Load-Outs

	F-16C	F-15E	B-1B	B-2	B-52H
General Purpose Bombs					
Mk-82	12	26	84	80	51
Mk-84	4	7	0	16	18
Cluster Bombs					
CBU-52,58,71	8	26	0	0	51
CBU-87	8	12	15	34	28
CBU-89	8	12	15	34	30
CBU-97	8	15	30	34	16 w/WCMD
Mk-20	8	26	0	0	24
Guided Munitions					
GBU-10	4	7	0	0	10
GBU-12	12	15	0	0	10
JDAM	4	5	24	16	12
JSOW	4	5	12	16	12
JASSM	2	3	24	16	12
WCMD	4	5	30	0	16

CBU - Cluster Bomb Unit
GBU - Guided Bomb Unit
JASSM - Joint Air-to-Surface Stand-off Missile
JDAM - Joint Direct Attack Munition
JSOW - Joint Stand-off Weapon
Mk - Mark (weapon version designator)
WCMD - Wind Corrected Munitions Dispenser

Bombers employing guided weapons can achieve multiple "point" kills per pass in contrast to the limited carriage of other platforms. Therefore, the capability of new munitions to achieve multiple kills per weapon and the ability to deliver multiple weapons per pass combine to bring a great deal of mass to bear very efficiently in terms of sortie requirements. As such, bombers contribute directly to another key principle of warfare -- economy of force. But the capabilities of our bomber force go well beyond discussions of firepower and mass. Range is a key consideration as well.

Range

Bombers embody the airpower tenant of range. Long-range aviation permits airpower to directly challenge an enemy at any depth, even from intercontinental ranges with very little response time. This capability to strike from great distances is a huge benefit as we transition to continental US (CONUS) force basing. In a crisis, their long range, coupled with speed, enables bombers to bring firepower to the scene very quickly. As the Strategic Aerospace Warfare Study Panel points out:

> The prevailing scenarios underlying current US military planning for major regional contingencies presume that the US will have sufficient warning to permit substantial deployments of American forces to overseas theaters prior to the beginning of hostilities. Potential aggressors, on the other hand, have powerful incentives, underscored by the outcome of the Gulf War, to deny the US such warning. If an aggressor manages to do so, then the ability of aerospace forces to bring precise, intense firepower to bear at global distances within *hours or days* [emphasis in original], as opposed to weeks or months, will be a far more precious commodity than it has been in the past.[2]

Furthermore, bombers provide strike options when theater basing rights are denied to aircraft with shorter "legs." Although the reader may point to the option of using carrier-based aviation in such circumstances, operational considerations may again prevail. For example, the target sets at hand might be attacked more economically or efficiently by bombers. In addition, target sets exist which are beyond the range of carrier air. As former Air Force Chief of Staff, Gen Ronald Fogleman stated, "There are parts of the world that are just not accessible by any other kind of force than long-range, intercontinental kinds of aircraft."[3] In these cases, the ability to employ bomber stand-off weapons with extreme ranges offers even more possibilities. In short, bombers offer the National Command Authorities (NCA) a wide set of crisis response options. However, in the nuclear deterrence arena, there are no alternatives to bombers.

Nuclear Operations

Bombers have a specific niche in the US Single Integrated Operations Plan (SIOP) which no other vehicle can fill. In contrast to other nuclear forces, bombers offer a very visible deterrent to nuclear aggression. Unlike the land- and sea-based legs of the TRIAD, bombers are extremely visible when generated in preparation for nuclear operations. The invisible nature of missiles may leave some doubt concerning US resolve in the minds of a potential aggressor, however, generating the bomber force to a nuclear posture is easily verified and removes all doubt about US resolve. In addition, some nuclear targets require high yield weapons and precise delivery. Bombers offer the accuracy and throw weight which missiles can't deliver when attacking hardened and buried targets.

In short, the range, speed, lethality, and precision of bombers combine to offer the US a multitude of employment options in crisis situations. No other land- or sea-based force offers this fusion of capabilities in a single platform. Bombers belong, and it behooves the Air Force to manage them wisely because, as history reveals, bombers are an indispensable tool in conflict.

Notes

[1] "Area-type" targets such as rail marshalling yards and petroleum production and storage facilities usually encompass several square miles and consist of numerous key elements designated as desired mean points of impact (DMPIs). Strike sorties must place a certain number of weapons within a specified distance of these DMPIs to achieve the

Notes

desired effect or level of damage. Forces such as troops in the open, armored columns, etc., also constitute an area target but lack specified DMPIs. In either case, it's often more efficient and economical to saturate the entire target area with dumb bombs than it is to target each specific DMPI or force element with a guided weapon.

[2] Strategic Aerospace Warfare Study Panel, *Aerospace Power for the 21st Century: A Theory to Fly By*, White Paper (Maxwell Air Force Base AL, 1996), 15.

[3] Gen Ronald R. Fogleman, chief of staff, US Air Force, address to The Toqueville Group, Capitol Hill, Washington, D.C., 13 September 1996.

Chapter 3

The Historical Perspective

Airpower's relatively brief history provides some insight into the roles, missions, and employment of bomber aircraft. For example, World War II (WWII) stands out as a case study in the use of bombers in the classic roles of strategic bombing and interdiction. However, since bombing doctrine was just coming of age in WWII, let's turn to post-WWII campaigns and operations to examine the historical roles, missions, and methods of employing bombardment forces.

Korea

The Korean war saw the employment of US B-26 Invader medium- and B-29 Super Fortress heavy-bombers in a variety of roles. However, the greatest contribution by bombers was through interdiction.

Immediately following the invasion of South Korea by northern forces, bombers began flying interdiction missions in June 1950. Due to a shortage of fighter-bomber assets in the theater, medium and heavy bombers continued to press interdiction attacks against armor, troop concentrations, and supply dumps. Simultaneously, B-29s began attacking strategic targets in the North including steel plants, oil depots, railway yards, and harbors. With MacAurthur's landing at Inchon and the destruction of key North Korean strategic targets by September, the bombers reverted to tactical bombing.[1]

With consolidation of the United Nations ground position by August 1951, bombers assumed responsibility for all interdiction in eastern and western Korea. But the enemy's use of night convoys and intense anti-aircraft fire in the low altitude interdiction environment forced the bombers into night operations. Equipped with spotlights or flares, C-47s operated in "hunter-killer" formations with B-26s flying in one- to three-mile trail. The tactic involved target illumination by the C-47 allowing the B-26, without a radar capable of tracking moving ground targets, to visually aim its weapons.[2] In addition to this innovative tactic, B-29s began employing 1,000lb. RAZON and 12,000lb. TARZON radio-guided bombs against key interdiction targets like bridges and storage areas.[3]

Utilizing both guided weapons and general purpose munitions, the bombers flew in excess of 76,000 sorties destroying over 38,000 vehicles, 4100 rail cars and locomotives, and 168 bridges in addition to 18 key industrial targets in the North. In all, over 80 percent of these bomber sorties were flown at night.[4]

During the Korean War, bombers focused on fairly classic missions. However, the US air campaigns during Vietnam offer a more unique outlook on bomber employment.

Vietnam

Vietnam saw extensive use of B-52 nuclear bombers converted for duty in conventional roles. Although B-52s took part in almost every operation in the air war over Vietnam, we'll focus on only three: *Rolling Thunder*, the siege of Khe Sanh, and *Linebacker II*.

Rolling Thunder

Rolling Thunder began in February 1965. *Rolling Thunder* was a systematic bombing campaign whose dominant objectives were strategic persuasion and interdiction of North Vietnamese support for the insurgency in the south.[5] At the heart of *Rolling Thunder* was a target list developed by the Joint Chiefs of Staff. The 94-target list, as it became known, contained infrastructure targets believed to be the most direct link to North Vietnam's (NVN's) war-making potential.[6] Implementation of the 94-target list included B-52 strikes on supply and storage sites, however, attacks on ports and the cities of Hanoi and Haiphong were prohibited in order to avoid civilian casualties and a widening of the war.[7] These initial strikes, flown from Guam, encompassed 15-hour missions covering over 5,500 miles.[8] Despite a tremendous level of effort, *Rolling Thunder* eventually ended in failure because the political and military strategies behind the campaign were ill-suited to a limited conflict against an enemy waging guerrilla war. Although this first use of B-52s in an interdiction role ended in failure, Vietnam did produce the first successful use of heavy bombers in a close support role.

Khe Sanh

B-52s participated in the successful defense of Khe Sanh during January 1968. Khe Sanh was a Marine air base located 20 miles south of the demilitarized zone (DMZ) separating North and South Vietnam. On 21 Jan, the North Vietnamese Army (NVA) attacked Khe Sanh after occupying the heights surrounding the base. From their commanding positions, the NVA laid siege to Khe Sanh for over two months. In order to ensure the survival of the Marine battalions trapped at Khe Sanh, US air forces responded with *Operation Niagara.*

Niagara began on 22 Jan when B-52s bombed surrounding NVA positions while C-130s and Marine helicopters resupplied and reinforced the besieged base. Then in February, the B-52 role expanded with *Operation Bugle Note.* Air planners divided the target areas around Khe Sanh into 1x2 km "kill boxes." Formations of B-52s saturated each of these kill boxes at 90-minute intervals, day and night, bombing as close as 1,000 yards from friendly forces. Following *Bugle Note*, B-52s kept the pressure on flying 48 sorties per day the rest of February and 444 sorties during March. All told, B-52s destroyed 274 NVA positions. The siege ended on 6 April 1968 culminating in the successful defense of Khe Sanh.[9] It would be another four years before bombers again played a decisive role in the Vietnam War.

Linebacker II

Linebacker II lasted from 18 to 29 December 1972. Its objective was to force the North to negotiate by maintaining a massive effort against their war-making capability and means of supply.[10] To convey this message to NVN, US air forces responded with a concentration of effort against "vital centers" to disrupt the North's economic, military, and political structure.[11]

Planners divided the air forces into two compressed operations: daylight raids consisting of fighter-bombers and night attacks using F-111s and B-52s. Each strike included complementary support elements providing fighter escort, electronic countermeasures (ECM), and suppression of enemy air defenses.[12] The general strategy

10

behind the night attacks entailed bomber strikes against rail yards, storage areas, power plants, communication centers, and airfields around Hanoi.[13]

In total, the Air Force lost 15 B-52s during the *Linebacker II* campaign. All of these losses resulted from surface-to-air missile (SAM) attacks which drove major changes to campaign tactics. After nine B-52 losses in the first three days of bombing, General Meyer, Commander of Strategic Air Command (SAC), reduced the B-52 sortie rate to 30 per day allowing only B-52Ds with upgraded ECM to fly strike missions.[14] SAC planners also varied bomber approach routings, altitudes, and post-target turns between each bomber cell.[15] Finally, Meyer ordered direct attacks against SAM storage facilities and launch sites in order to curb losses.[16] After implementing these changes on Day Five of the campaign and resuming normal sortie rates, the Air Force lost only four more B-52s. This change in tactics not only cut the loss rate, but yielded an additional dividend as well.

On the day after Christmas, bombers began an all-out attack on air defenses designed to preclude further B-52 losses. With air defenses down, B-52s could then strike at will putting the North at the mercy of the US.[17] Saturating the northern air defenses and the bombing of SAM sites and storage facilities proved very effective. By Day Eleven, NVN had depleted their SAM supply leaving them defenseless and eager to negotiate.[18] After the Day 11 strikes, attacks above the 20th parallel came to a halt and the peace process began in earnest.[19]

During 11 days of combat in *Linebacker II*, B-52s flew 739 sorties and delivered 15,237 tons of ordinance on 34 target complexes.[20] Though costly, the campaign fulfilled its political objectives through a massive dose of strategic attack using B-52s coupled

11

with effective force packages. The next successful US air campaign occurred almost 20 years later.

Desert Storm

The *Desert Storm* air campaign against Iraq kicked off at 0300 on 17 January 1991 after a six-month buildup of coalition forces in the region. Ironically, the first strike aircraft to launch lifted off the day prior at 0636 from Barksdale AFB, LA. In all, seven B-52s departed Barksdale on the morning of 16 Jan to deliver thirty-five AGM-86C cruise missiles against Iraqi communications, power generation, and transmission facilities.[21] These opening strategic shots of the Gulf War constituted only 1.4% of the force structure used on the first day of the war while encompassing 100% of the Day One strikes against electric power generation facilities.[22] These strikes embodied the Air Force doctrine behind *Global Reach, Global Power*, but were only the beginning of an air campaign that used bombers in a wide variety of roles and employment scenarios.

B-52s performed other missions on the first night as well. While the cruise missile strikes were in progress, other bombers pounded telecommunications facilities and command, control, and communications (C^3) nodes in a strategic attack role. Likewise, B-52s performed offensive counter-air missions. Using low-level tactics and 1,000lb. runway busting munitions, three-ship formations struck all major Iraqi forward operating air bases near the Saudi border. These attacks kept the Iraqi Air Force from forward deploying their fighters and threatening coalition E-3A AWACS and tankers in refueling orbits.[23] Finally, the first day of the war concluded with low-level strikes by seven B-52s against the Tawakalna Division of the Republican Guard in a direct attack role.[24]

After the first three days of the war, B-52s abandoned the low altitude tactic for high altitude strikes free from the threat of anti-aircraft artillery (AAA). For the rest of the campaign, the bombers performed interdiction missions and strategic attacks against key facilities such as the Bayji oil refinery, manufacturing sites in the Tikrit area, the Taji missile repair facility, and the Tarmiya nuclear production facility. These high altitude sorties, coupled with extended enroute times from bases as far away as Diego Garcia, presented unique challenges for the crews. One of the most frequent challenges was target changes. Fully 25% of the missions received new targets while enroute as a function of the rapidly changing nature of the war and long transit times to Iraq.[25] High altitude operations created other problems as well. SAC wings came to the war prepared to fight at low altitude with high-drag munitions. Switching to high altitude tactics, SAC units found themselves with very few conical fins available for the B-52's general purpose weapon of choice, the M-117 750lb. bomb.[26] As a work-around in the face of these shortages, munitions builders banded retarded M-117 high-drag fins in the closed position so the weapon could be released from high altitude. This had a drastic effect on weapon ballistics and led to many of the complaints concerning bombing accuracy voiced after the war.

During the course of the war, several unique missions evolved for the bombers. These missions included minefield breaching actions, "SCUD hunting" to counter the growing ballistic missile threat, and "leaflet bombing" in order to demoralize the Republican Guard divisions.[27] But by far, the most decisive use of the B-52 during the Gulf War was direct attack of fielded Iraqi ground forces. Beginning on the first day of the war, three-ships of bombers attacked Iraqi divisions around the clock every three hours.[28] These attacks caused the complete demoralization of the ground forces and led to the mass desertions and surrenders that occurred during the ground offensive.[29] The B-52s were so effective in this role that in the final phases of the air campaign, any attempts to target the bombers outside Kuwait met strong resistance from Central Command (CENTCOM) leadership.[30]

All of this is not to say that *Desert Storm* bomber operations were perfect. Post-war after-action reports revealed the warts. General Butler, Commander In Chief of SAC at the time, offered the sharpest criticism of B-52 performance. Concerning bomber deployability, he stated that SAC:

> ...was not as prepared for rapid deployment and conventional missions...in Desert Storm as we could have been...going into the Gulf War, SAC's readiness spares kits were rated overall Not Mission Capable.[31]

Other criticisms levied against the bombers concerned the lack of available bomber bases in theater. This meant that 75% of the wings that deployed for the war had to routinely fly 14- to 16-hour missions which, in turn, limited their ability to generate combat sorties. Likewise, the B-52's lack of PGM capability (although some B-52s did have the capability to launch AGM-142 precision stand-off missiles) severely constrained the choice of bomber targets. And finally, the B-52's lack of stealth required it to be packaged with force protection assets.[32]

Overall, the 74 B-52Gs that participated in the Gulf War flew 1,624 sorties and dropped 25,700 tons of munitions. These figures represent over 30% of the total of all US bombs dropped and over twice the tonnage dropped by all six carrier battle groups in the entire Gulf War.[33] The bomber once again brought mass to the fight and proved it's worth in a modern air campaign, but the unique missions and shortcomings documented above provide some serious food for thought concerning future operations. One final air operation provides some further insight.

Desert Strike

The last air operation worth examining is the *Desert Strike* operation of 1996. Although very little information concerning the operation is in print, and many of the details remain classified, *Desert Strike* offers some important implications for bomber operations.

Fearing collusion between the Iraqi government and the Kurdistan Democratic Party aimed at exterminating the Patriotic Union of Kurdistan, National Command Authorities ordered the deployment of bombers to Andersen AFB, Guam. In response, three B-52s departed Barksdale AFB on 31 August 1996. The aircraft, due to the 16-hour flight and time change, recovered on Guam early on 2 Sep. Within 18 hours after landing, two B-52s were back in the air making their way toward Iraqi targets with AGM-86C cruise missiles.[34]

Even though the bombers transited airspace belonging to two theater commanders (CINCs) and the bomber targets lay well inside Iraq and the CENTCOM theater of operations, the B-52s never "chopped" operational control from 8th Air Force to CENTCOM. This created a miserable situation for the aircrews from a command and control (C^2) perspective. As targets changed at the direction of National Command Authorities, the crews were tasked directly by the 8th Air Force commander who, by all rights, should not even have had operational control at this point. The bomber crews lay

15

at the receiving end of this convoluted chain trying to perform target changes with a fairly inflexible missile system designed for nuclear operations. Only the skill of the deployed aircrews and a few key unit representatives augmenting theater CINC staffs kept *Desert Strike* from falling on its face.

With the completion of *Desert Strike*, the B-52s covered almost 16,000 air miles after 34 hours of flight.[35] Despite the adversity created by the C^2 situation, the bombers without ever penetrating enemy airspace, successfully launched 13 cruise missiles targeting SAM sites and air defense radars. Considering the ineffectiveness of these strikes and the irrelevancy of the targets attacked, *Desert Strike* was a military failure. However, in the politicians' eyes, *Desert Strike* was a startling success as it provided a means of demonstrating national resolve without risking US aircrews. As such, *Desert Strike* cruise missile attacks may be a dubious forerunner for new bomber employment methods in regional contingencies, however, the Air Force has a long way to go in implementing the C^2 architecture required to execute these Global Power missions.

Summary of Historical Trends

In terms of requirements, this brief historical reflection on bomber operations provides significant food for thought. In the 50 years following WWII, bombers performed almost every conceivable airpower mission.

History indicates that the application of bombers in strategic attack and interdiction roles are a consistent trend. The bomber's inherent range, and payload are well suited to these missions. However, history also reveals the bomber to be a fairly flexible platform capable of adapting to missions such as close air support and forms of psychological operations. More recent examples such as the use of bombers in SCUD hunting and minefield breaching operations during *Desert Storm* points to the continued adaptation of bombers to evolving warfare. Likewise, *Desert Strike* indicates that bombers, armed with long-range stand-off munitions, may play an increased role in quick reaction political strikes against our enemies. In addition to roles and missions, history points to consistent trends in the employment of bombers. Chief among these trends are increased deployability; large stables of adaptable munitions; and the need for training programs emphasizing night operations, composite force integration, and flexibility. The following table summarizes these factors.

Table 2. Summation of Historical Requirements

Source	Mission	Requirement			
		Avionics	**Weaponry**	**Logistics**	**Training**
Korea	Strategic Attack Interdiction	Off-board targeting	Need for PGMs	High sortie rates	Night operations
Vietnam	Strategic Attack Interdiction CAS Psychological Operations		Area targets Large bomb loads Need for PGMs	High sortie rates	Long-range ops Package ops Kill boxes

Source	Mission	Requirement			
		Avionics	**Weaponry**	**Logistics**	**Training**
Desert Storm	Strategic Attack Interdiction		Flexible munitions Need for	Deployment High sortie rates	Long-range ops High-altitude ops

	OCA Mine Breaching SCUD Hunting Psychological Operations		PGMs Cratering munitions Area targets		Force integration Target changes
Desert Strike	Coercion	Command and control	Flexible targeting Stand-off munitions	Deployment	Long-range ops Target changes

With these historical trends in mind, let's move on to an examination of current strategy and doctrine guidance to further define bomber requirements.

Notes

[1] Victor Flintham, *Air Wars and Aircraft: A Detailed Record of Air Combat, 1945 to the Present* (New York: Facts on File, 1990), 228-229.

[2] Robert F. Futrell, *The United States Air Force in Korea, 1950-1953* (Washington, D.C.: Office of Air Force History, 1983), 325-331.

[3] Futrell, 318-323.

[4] Flintham, 230.

[5] Earl H. Tilford, Jr. *Setup: What the Air Force Did in Vietnam and Why* (Maxwell Air Force Base AL: Air University Press, 1991), 104.

[6] Gen William W. Momyer, *Air Power in Three Wars* (Washington, D.C.: US Government Printing Office, 1978), 15.

[7] Flintham, 269.

[8] Flintham, 270.

[9] Flintham, 271-272.

[10] Karl J. Eschmann, *LINEBACKER: The Untold Story of the Air Raids Over North Vietnam* (New York: Ballantine Books, 1989), 3.

[11] Momyer, 33.

[12] Eschmann, 4.

[13] Mark Clodfelter, *The Limits of Airpower: The American Bombing of North Vietnam* (New York: The Free Press, 1989), 184.

[14] Eschmann, 140.

[15] Eschmann, 138.

[16] Clodfelter, 187.

[17] Tilford, 259.

[18] Eschmann, 213.

Notes

[19] Eschmann, 192.

[20] Tilford, 263.

[21] Richard P. Hallion, *Storm Over Iraq: Air Power and the Gulf War* (Washington, D.C.: Smithsonian Institution Press, 1992), 162-163.

[22] *Gulf War Air Power Survey (GWAPS), Volume II, Part I, Operations* (Washington, D.C.: Government Printing Office, 1993), 142.

[23] *GWAPS, Vol II, Part I,* 134.

[24] *GWAPS, Vol II, Part I,* 144.

[25] James A. Winnefeld, Preston Niblack, and Dana J. Johnson, *A League of Airmen: US Air Power in the Gulf War* (Santa Monica CA: RAND Project Air Force, 1994), 168.

[26] Winnefeld, 233.

[27] *GWAPS, Vol II, Part I,* 177-324.

[28] *GWAPS, Vol II, Part I,* 225.

[29] Hallion, 218.

[30] *GWAPS, Volume II, Part II, Effects and Effectiveness* (Washington, D.C.: Government Printing Office, 1993), 99.

[31] Winnefeld, 46.

[32] Winnefeld, 256.

[33] Hallion, 218.

[34] Terry Somerville, "B-52s Lead Attack on Iraq," *Air Force News Service*, 5 September 1996.

[35] Somerville.

Chapter 4

Requirements from the Top-Down

In the previous chapter we established historical trends concerning application of bombers from a perspective of roles, missions, and employment. Now we move to an examination of current guidance to establish on-going requirements. In performing this examination, we'll start at the top with our National Security Strategy and progress down through doctrine and operational strategy documents.

Any requirements definition process should logically start at the highest level of national planning guidance. The current requirements process at Air Combat Command (ACC) does just that. In order to define requirements for specific weapons systems, ACC's utilizes a strategy to task analysis process which begins with the National Security Strategy. It then refines these requirements by tracing through the National Military Strategy, Theater Concept of Operations (ConOps), and operational objectives. At this point, the process defines tasks necessary to accomplish those objectives and, in the end, these tasks define the features and characteristics (requirements) of various weapons systems.[1]

Figure 1. Strategy to Task Hierarchy

The whole modernization and planning process is very thorough and sound for major conflict at the theater-level, however, it's grounded in analysis of threats and weapon applications at the tactical level. As such, the system fails to address the full spectrum of conflict, neglects a wide range of considerations involving the entire array of bomber missions, and completely ignores the nature of future conflict. To address the full scope of potential conflict and associated missions in our own requirements definition process we need to re-look requirements from a top-down perspective.

National Security Strategy

From a macro view, the 1997 National Security Strategy (NSS) provides first insight to the overarching capabilities required of our forces. In support of national core objectives, the NSS states that we must strengthen our military tools to counter growing threats to security. Furthermore, we must be able to:

> ...respond to the full spectrum of potential crises and prepare against future threats. Our military forces will have the ability to respond to challenges short of war, and in concert with regional friends and allies, to win two overlapping major theater wars.[2]

The NSS warns that increases in technology make state-centered and transnational threats such as weapons of mass destruction (WMDs) like nuclear, biological, and chemical (NBC) weapons more lethal to our forces. The NSS, in turn, identifies military force and the credible threat of its use as an essential ingredient in preserving our national safety. If necessary, we must be able to act either in a coalition or unilaterally to decisively defeat these threats. This requires forces to be capable of performing multiple missions and to train with multiple missions in mind.[3]

These multiple missions entail the ability to react at all levels of the conflict spectrum. The NSS specifically requires that we maintain the ability to respond at every level from humanitarian assistance to nuclear war. At the theater level, the NSS directs US forces to maintain the ability to seize the initiative and minimize territory lost before we halt an aggressor's invasion, be prepared to fight against asymmetric means such as chemical or information attack, and be prepared to rapidly withdraw from small-scale contingencies to fight at the theater level. At the far end of the spectrum, we must maintain a strong nuclear deterrent posture to deter hostile foreign governments.[4]

National Military Strategy

This broad guidance is refined in our National Military Strategy (NMS). The NMS provides strategic direction for the armed forces in implementing the President's NSS. In preparing to meet perceived threats, the NMS lays out our national military objectives as promoting peace and stability and, when necessary, decisively defeating our adversaries. Maintaining credible nuclear and conventional forces capable of deterring or defeating "nearly simultaneous large-scale, cross-border aggression in two distant theaters in overlapping time frames" is the key element of strategy identified to meet those objectives. In addition, the NMS states that we must be able to conduct several small-scale contingencies at the same time and be able to respond at all levels across the conflict spectrum.[5]

From these elements of strategy the NMS identifies four strategic concepts governing the use of joint conventional forces. The first of these is strategic agility which is the ability to concentrate, employ, and sustain forces anywhere at a speed and tempo unmatched by our enemies. Next is overseas presence -- the positioning of forces in key regions of the world as a visible deterrent and hedge against unforeseen aggression. In turn, power projection is the ability to rapidly deploy and sustain tailored force packages to dispersed locations in crisis theaters. Finally, the NMS defines decisive force as the use of military power to overwhelm any adversary and achieve conflict resolution in terms favorable to our nation.[6]

The last area of the NMS pertinent to our discussion of bomber requirements is the characteristics of forces. These include multi-mission capability, jointness, and interoperability. In short, our forces must be highly trained, mobile, and capable of performing a variety of missions at all levels conflict, even while under attack from asymmetric threats. Likewise, these forces must be seamless and capable of smooth integration into both joint and combined operations.[7]

Thus far, national-level documents have defined requirements in broad, generic terms. Joint publications go another level deeper in defining specific roles and requirements.

Joint Pubs

Joint Publication 1, *Joint Warfare of the Armed Forces of the United States*, defines some of the missions and force requirements necessary to implement the NMS. Specifically, Joint Pub 1 enumerates air and maritime superiority, direct attack of enemy centers of gravity, and exploitation of the information differential as key tasks in executing joint campaigns. Air and maritime superiority are essential to effectively project and sustain power. Superiority in these two realms also permits freedom of action for our forces. Likewise, attacks on centers of gravity, both near and deep, are integral to the joint campaign. Simultaneous attacks on leadership, infrastructure, and fielded forces lead to paralysis which maximizes the combined effect of our joint forces. Finally, joint forces exploiting their superior access to information, are able to operate at strategic, operational, and tactical levels at a pace exceeding the ability of the enemy to respond effectively.[8]

From a requirements standpoint, Joint Pub 1 puts emphasis on logistics, all-source intelligence, force integration, agility, and sustainability.[9] Logistics and sustainability go hand-in-hand providing the ability to get to the theater quickly and then mount and support prolonged operations. Similarly, the fusion of intelligence enables commanders and their forces to integrate and employ, striking with speed and mass throughout the depth of the theater. Agility provides the flexibility to move from one mission, operation, or theater to the next before our enemy can mount an effective defense or attack.

Joint Publication 3-0, *Doctrine for Joint Operations*, addresses the operational requirements. At the operational level, joint force commanders employ and use the elements of operational art. The elements of operational art that apply to bomber requirements are:[10]

- Synergy – integration and synchronization of forces
- Simultaneity and Depth – bringing force to bear on the enemy's entire structure in a simultaneous manner
- Anticipation – remaining alert for opportunities to exploit the situation
- Leverage – gaining, maintaining, and exploiting advantages in combat power across the spectrum
- Timing and Tempo – conducting operations at a tempo and point in time that exploits friendly capabilities and inhibits the enemy
- Operational Reach and Approach – basing conditions that allow forces to deliver symmetric and asymmetric blows with power and ferocity
- Forces and Functions – defeating either enemy forces, functions, or both
- Centers of Gravity – massing effect against enemy sources of power

Synergy demands bombers and crews that are equipped and trained to integrate with other joint and combined forces. Simultaneity and Depth as well as Leverage, Forces and Functions, and Centers of Gravity all require flexible weaponry capable of holding a wide spectrum of targets at risk. Anticipation and Timing/Tempo stipulate that bombers incorporate avionics capable of enhancing aircrew situational awareness and accessing data from off-board intelligence sources and flexible targeting platforms. Simple, reliable, and efficient C^2 architecture and equipment is also necessary to achieve all of these elements. Finally, Operational Reach and Approach requires logistics infrastructures and processes capable of rapidly mounting and sustaining operations over any distance, whether deployed or operating from CONUS. As we're about to see, all of these characteristics fall directly in line with concepts found in Air Force doctrine.

Air Force Doctrine

Air Force Doctrine Document 1, *Air Force Basic Doctrine*, lays out the guiding principles, tenets, and core competencies of the USAF. While the principles of war are the same as those put forth in all joint and service doctrine, the USAF core competencies form the heart of the Air Force perspective of warfare. The Air Force core competencies are:[11]

- Rapid Global Mobility
- Precision Engagement
- Global Attack
- Air and Space Superiority
- Information Superiority
- Agile Combat Support

Bombers directly contribute to, or embody, three of these core competencies: Rapid Global Mobility, Precision Engagement, and Global Attack. Increasing bomber effectiveness in these core competencies correspondingly increases their utility in achieving the objectives laid out in joint doctrine and national strategies. Similarly, two core competencies, Information Superiority and Agile Combat Support, are empowering capabilities for bomber forces. Increasing bomber capacity to utilize these competencies, in turn, makes them more effective combat forces.

Air Force Basic Doctrine also enumerates the basic functions of airpower. The functions executed by bomber forces are:[12]

- Counterair (Offensive Counterair)

- Counterland (Interdiction, Close Air Support)
- Countersea
- Strategic Attack
- Counterinformation (Offensive Counterinformation)
- Surveillance (maritime)

In addition, bomber forces utilize the following air and space power functions.[13]

- Counterair (Offensive and Defensive Counterair)
- Counterinformation (Offensive and Defensive Counterinformation)
- Command and Control
- Airlift
- Air Refueling
- Special Operations Employment
- Intelligence
- Surveillance
- Reconnaissance
- Combat Search and Rescue
- Navigation and Positioning
- Weather Services

Maximizing the bombers' capacity to execute each of these functions and, at the same time, maximizing their ability to utilize the enabling functions, increases the overall effectiveness of the bomber force. Based on these broad missions and requirements generated from our top-down perspective, it's time to see how the bombers stack up.

Summary of Top-Down Requirements

From this chapter we can develop the following table as a means of summarizing top-down requirements. Notice the nature of missions driven by this perspective. All require high mobility; agility; and flexibility in terms of avionics, munitions, and training.

Table 3. Summation of Top-Down Requirements

		Requirement			
Source	Mission	Avionics	Weaponry	Logistics	Training
NSS	Nuclear Deterrence	Command and control	Security	Reconstitution	Nuclear environment

27

	Conventional Operations	Secure comms	Flexible munitions Anti-WMD	Agility Deployability	Flexibility Interoperability NBC threat
NMS	Nuclear Deterrence Conventional Operations	Command and control Secure comms	Security Flexible munitions	Reconstitution Agility Deployability Sustainment	Nuclear environment Flexibility Package ops Joint ops NBC threat
Joint Pubs	Strategic Attack Maritime Control	Command and control Intel fusion Situational awareness	Flexible targeting Flexible munitions	Deployability Sustainment High sortie rates Agility	Joint ops Combined ops
AFDD-1	Counterair Counterland Countersea Strategic Attack Counterinfo Surveillance	Command and control Secure comms Information fusion	Flexible targeting PGMs	Deployability Sustainment High sortie rates Agility	Package ops Global operations

Notes

[1] Headquarters Air Combat Command, *Air Combat Command Modernization Planning Process*, Director of Requirements briefing, Langley Air Force Base VA, 1997.

[2] *A National Security Strategy for a New Century* (Washington, D.C.: The White House, 1997), 5.

[3] *A National Security Strategy for a New Century*, 5-12.

[4] *A National Security Strategy for a New Century*, 9-13.

[5] The Joint Chiefs of Staff, "National Military Strategy: Shape, Respond, Prepare Now -- A Military Strategy for a New Era," *Defense Technical Information Center*, 1997, n.p.; on-line, world wide web, 16 December 1997.

[6] Ibid.

Notes

[7] Ibid.

[8] The Joint Chiefs of Staff, *Joint Pub 1: Joint Warfare of the Armed Forces of the United States* (Washington, D.C.: US Government Printing Office, 10 January 1995), IV-7 - IV-9.

[9] Joint Pub 1, III-1 – IV-12.

[10] The Joint Chiefs of Staff, *Joint Pub 3-0: Doctrine for Joint Operations* (Washington, D.C.: US Government Printing Office, 1 February 1995), III-9 – III-24.

[11] Headquarters, Air Force Doctrine Center, *Air Force Doctrine Document 1: Air Force Basic Doctrine* (Maxwell Air Force Base AL, September 1997), 27-35.

[12] *Air Force Doctrine Document 1*, 45-60.

[13] Ibid.

Chapter 5

Back to the Future

The past is of no importance. The present is of no importance. It is with the future that we have to deal.

--Oscar Wilde

Although ACC's Modernization Planning Process does a good job of matching capabilities to current threats and missions, it's major flaw is its failure to look down the road toward future conflict. In our own requirements definition process we will address guidance contained in "future studies" and "vision documents."

Alternate Futures for 2025

In this study directed by the Chief of Staff of the Air Force, members of an Air University research team attempted to define the concepts, capabilities, and technology required for the USAF to remain a dominant force in the future. By identifying major drivers affecting the shape of world progress, the team postulated four futures at the extremes of a three dimensional model. This model used the degree of American interaction in world affairs; the extent of technology proliferation; and the distribution of economic, political, and military power as variables in the evolution of world affairs. We'll briefly explore each of these four extreme worlds to help define required capabilities.[1]

Gulliver's Travails

This future is characterized by dispersed world power, extensive US involvement in world affairs, and technology concentrated in a few select nations. Although technology continued to grow at an evolutionary rate with the US retaining its lead in space power, regulatory policies such as taxes and tariffs resulted in a future of technological haves and have-nots. The primary dangers to US national interests are therefore regional instability and transnational terrorism.[2]

In order to counter these threats, the US military must maintain a wide range of capabilities. Forces must react quickly and function across the entire spectrum of conflict from peace operations to nuclear deterrence. Light, mobile US forces must be able to deploy rapidly to crisis scenes and utilize their information superiority to counter threats in the region. These forces also must maintain a minimal theater footprint to avoid targeting by enemy forces using weapons of mass destruction. Likewise, our forces must be prepared to operate in biological and chemical environments. Rapidly responding, highly survivable platforms with precision targeting capability are the key to successful military operations in the world of *Gulliver's Travails*.[3]

Zaibatsu

In contrast to *Gulliver's Travails*, *Zaibatsu* is a future dominated by corporations. As such, world power is greatly dispersed and technological growth is exponential. Since most conflict results from competition for markets and resources between the dominant corporations, US national involvement in world affairs is constrained. The US, however, supplies the bulk of the United Nation's security forces used to maintain a relatively peaceful world. Forces rarely act independently since economic interdependence is the

primary stabilizer of relations.[4]

The greatest challenge to US forces in *Zaibatsu* is enemies armed with modern,

sophisticated weaponry. Information warfare and data security are also prime areas of

concern. The major battle for the military other than embargo and sanction enforcement

is the fight for relevancy in this rather benign future.[5]

Digital Cacophony

This future is a world completely transformed by technology. It's also a world very

susceptible to random violence with dispersed world power and global US involvement.

Given the technical and physical instability of this future, the US national security

strategy focuses on defending the nation against hostile actions including the use of

WMDs and ensuring the security of US information channels.[6]

The emphasis of this national security strategy demands technically advanced and

highly mobile military forces. These forces must be proficient at fighting across the

spectrum of conflict, extremely versatile, and armed with flexible weaponry.

Reconnaissance, detection, and communications are key technologies vital to the success

of US forces in a rapidly evolving information environment.[7]

King Khan

King Khan is the most challenging future for the US. This future is dominated by an

Asian superpower while US world power has declined due to economic problems. *King

Khan* features world power concentrated in Asia, constrained technological growth, and

constrained US involvement in world affairs. The US has lost its technological dominance and its forces have declined significantly due to fiscal constraints. In contrast, the Asian superpower can afford a huge military. Since the US is not strong enough to act alone, national security strategy dictates that the US achieve security through alliances. In addition, the US has again adopted a strategy of Mutual Assured Destruction provided solely by ICBMs to ensure its survival. Military force capabilities are limited to humanitarian operations, counterterrorism, and anti-drug activity. At the regional level, US military forces wage war using *mujahadeen* tactics.[8]

These four futures represent the extremes in world development and are intended to eliminate surprise. However, the Air Force Chief of Staff directed development of one more potential future – one less extreme and somewhat more relevant. This future is a compromise of the three driving factors and serves as an intermediate crossroad to the more extreme futures.

2015 Crossroads

This world is a waypoint to the other futures. Technological change is somewhat constrained due to budgetary pressure while US involvement in world affairs remains robust. World power remains somewhat concentrated, but is beginning to disperse. The US, Russia, and China dominate the world. In this tripolar world, the US fights to maintain its technological edge while fostering the stable development of Russia and China. Vital interests include continued American prosperity and maintaining the free flow of oil from the Persian Gulf.[9]

This future demands US forces that are flexible and mobile. Specifically, they must be able to deploy easily on short notice and sustain operations for up to nine months out of a year. Once deployed, forces must be capable of maintaining high operations tempos and rapidly shifting from one theater to another. Thus, logistics processes must be fully capable of supporting these operations relying heavily on prepositioned equipment and information systems. Likewise, the force footprint must remain as small as possible to limit the exposure of personnel to threats such as WMDs. Furthermore, US forces must rely on new information systems for reconnaissance, signals intelligence, and targeting. All of this must be done with existing weapons systems and a limited modernization effort due to budgetary constraints.[10]

Alternate Futures for 2025 provides a very broad look at potential futures for military employment. In many cases these futures are much too broad to be of much value. In contrast, Col. Jeffery R. Barnett offers simplified view of future conflict.

Future War

In his book *Future War: An Assessment of Aerospace Campaigns in 2010*, Col. Barnett divides future conflict into two scenarios: those against peer competitors and those against niche competitors. He defines peer competitors as nations capable of fielding many types of emerging and current weapon systems in large numbers, tying their employment together in a concept of operations capitalizing on their mix of weapons. The peer competitor will be in direct competition with the US, seeking to capture a vital US interest and then defeating the US response to their aggression. A niche competitor, on the other hand, is a state, or states, fielding limited numbers of emerging weapons in combination with large inventories of current weapons. The niche competitor also develops a concept of operations to employ his weapons but does not achieve the full potential of his weapons mix. The niche competitor being militarily inferior to the US attempts to challenge US interests in a theater through conflict too costly for the US to bear.[11]

In combating peer competitors armed with state-of-the-art weapons, Col. Barnett provides a series of operational concepts critical to the success of US forces. The concepts applicable to bomber forces are:[12]

- Integration of intelligence, surveillance, and reconnaissance (ISR) systems
- Support for the information campaign
- Conducting offensive strikes within the enemy homeland
- Attacking enemy invasion/occupation forces
- Avoiding deployment of critical targets within range of enemy stealth

These operational concepts entail a wide range of activity. Integration of ISR assets fuses data collected by space-based, unmanned atmospheric, and manned atmospheric vehicles. By integrating imagery and intelligence functions, operators are able to tap the unique capabilities of any platform they deem necessary to identify threats and targets while eliminating enemy spoofing. While US forces enjoy dominant battlefield awareness provided by ISR integration, we must also deny the same to the enemy. By delivering munitions against critical information nodes identified by the Joint Force Information Component Commander (JFICC), bombers support the information campaign. Likewise, our forces must train to operate in corrupt information environments. Bombers will also conduct traditional attacks against the enemy homeland and his forces. These attacks must be weighed against political restrictions and may involve the use of nonlethal weapons which cripple enemy capabilities without the destruction that leads an enemy to resort to the use of WMDs. In attacking maneuvering enemy forces with brilliant munitions, bombers must rely on phased-array radar with moving target indicator supplied by either on-board systems or off-board sensors.

Attacks on enemy logistics centers and lines of communication require the use both cruise missiles and new cluster bomb units. While performing these operations, bombers will rely on their range to keep main bases out of range of enemy attack. As in our historical examples, this dictates long duration sorties and increases the likelihood of retasking strike missions while enroute. Finally, deployed operations will require bomber forces to trim their airlift requirements to fit within a finite ton-mile/day capacity.[13]

Engaging niche competitors will require many of the same operations as those conducted against a peer competitor. However, Col. Barnett points out the following additional concepts which bombers may execute or utilize.[14]

- Paralyzing enemy command and control
- Dominate battlefield awareness
- Attacking enemy wealth
- Supporting the ground counteroffensive

C^2 nodes, being critical to a niche competitor, are vulnerable to detection and attack. Once destroyed by bombers using precise munitions, US forces can act inside the niche competitor's decision cycle by conducting parallel attacks to disrupt and paralyze his operations. A necessary precursor to effective parallel attack is possessing dominant battlefield awareness. Although battlefield awareness is dependant on ISR integration discussed earlier, the critical aspect of obtaining awareness is getting reliable data directly to the user requiring the information -- in our case, mission planners and flight crews in the cockpit. Information must be broadcast, relayed, and received by systems utilizing large bandwidths and digital compression technology. Once armed with dominant battlefield awareness, bombers can effectively carry out attacks on enemy forces as well as attacks on enemy wealth. The goal in this case is to attack the supporting infrastructure which drives the enemy economy. A large stable of varied munitions are necessary to effectively deal with such a huge array of targets which includes transportation, industry, electrical production, communications, etc. Finally, after crippling the enemy's C^2, infrastructure, and support, bombers must be capable of aiding US ground forces in their counteroffensive. By using airpower, our bombers can efficiently shred what's left of enemy ground forces with general purpose, smart, and brilliant weapons to reduce the cost of a ground campaign in terms of US lives.[15]

All of these operational concepts fit squarely within the constructs of our primary vision documents: *Joint Vision 2010 (JV 2010)* and the Air Force's *Global Engagement*.

Joint Vision 2010

JV 2010, published by the Chairman of the Joint Chiefs of Staff, serves as a conceptual framework for guiding US services in developing the forces and doctrinal foundations to meet the challenges of an uncertain future. It defines the operational concepts necessary to provide our forces with Full Spectrum Dominance and thus achieve enduring US goals and national interests. The operational concepts follow.[16]

- Dominant Maneuver
- Precision Engagement
- Full Dimensional Protection
- Focused Logistics

These concepts are all based on assumptions about future force employment. Specifically, future operations will be joint, involving coalitions if possible, and will rely on our ability to project power, our superior training and the technological edge possessed by our forces. This technological edge encompasses long-range precision strike capability, a broad range of weapons effects, stealth, and integration of information systems. As such, bombers can achieve, employ, or benefit from every one of *JV 2010's* operational concepts.[17]

By the very definition of Dominant Maneuver, bombers can attack centers of gravity at any depth to force the enemy into a disadvantageous position or compel him to quit.[18] Dominant Maneuver makes direct use of the bomber's range, massed firepower, and varied weapons loads to efficiently achieve campaign objectives. However, bomber crews will require extensive data link capability, superior targeting systems, and upgraded weaponry to attain situational awareness and achieve the desired level of operational effect.

Likewise, bombers can employ the concept of Precision Engagement. Precision Engagement is not simply a reference to the employment of PGMs; more broadly, it entails the timely, appropriate, and precise application of bomber forces. If properly supported by a responsive C^2 architecture and information systems, bombers can deliver the appropriate munitions in sufficient quantity at the right time and place to generate the desired operational effect.[19] This too entails superior information data link and targeting capabilities as well as a varied array of weapons. In addition, bombers supported by either on- or off-board strike assessment systems usually have sufficient endurance to reengage a target if necessary. Using these same systems, loitering bombers can provide on-call strikes against a wide array of targets or pop-up threats.

Bombers benefit from, as well as contribute to, Full-Dimensional Protection. Obviously, bomber operations are more efficient if bases are free from attack, or at least enjoy advanced attack warning. Likewise, freedom from defensive enemy air action and ground defenses are absolutely crucial to the success of bomber missions. Although bombers retain the ability for limited self-protection, integration with force protection packages, even in the case of stealthy aircraft, is often essential. Integration with offensive counter air and surface threat suppression forces requires extensive training and very capable communications systems. Data link capability also enhances the ability of the aircrew to achieve situational awareness concerning threats, weather, and the disposition of both friendly and enemy air and ground forces. In an offensive sense, bombers contribute to Full-Dimensional Protection by attacking the enemy's ability to threaten our forces. Offensive counter air attacks against enemy airfields; destruction of ballistic missile production, logistics, and launch facilities; and elimination of enemy WMD production sites are just a few examples of offensive applications of bombers in this role. However, bombers will require information support and the appropriate weapons to affect these missions.

Lastly, bombers directly benefit from Focused Logistics. The fusion of information and transportation technology makes it possible for bombers to deploy quickly and sustain operations at the required tempo.[20] However, in the future bomber forces must reduce the size of their "support tail." Limited airlift resources will be unable to adequately support bomber forces under current deployment schemes. Bomber units must cut the size of their deployment packages and become more efficient in deployed logistics operations.

Bombers are fully capable of carrying out or contributing to the operations concepts proposed in *Joint Vision 2010*. The same is true of the core competencies embodied by the Air Force's vision document, *Global Engagement*.

Global Engagement

Global Engagement: A Vision for the 21ˢᵗ Century Air Force is the Department of the Air Force vision piece. It dovetails with the operational constructs laid out in *JV 2010* by outlining the air and space capabilities required to prevail in turn of the century conflict.

At the heart of *Global Engagement* are assumptions concerning the nature of 21ˢᵗ century warfare. Chief among these assumptions are the unpredictable nature of our enemies including the potential use of terrorist and NBC attacks, global proliferation of technology, the likelihood of conflict in urban areas and difficult terrain, information warfare, and the increasing need to operate from a power projection footing. The evolving nature of conflict gives way to six core competencies which are the essential functions of air and space power. These competencies present Joint Force Commanders with a tool box to employ in executing their campaign plans. The Air Force core competencies are:[21]

- Air and Space Superiority
- Global Attack
- Rapid Global Mobility
- Precision Engagement
- Information Superiority
- Agile Combat Support

Bombers contribute to or benefit from each of these competencies just as they do the operational concepts set forth in *JV 2010*. For example, Air and Space Superiority is the fundamental capability that prevents adversaries from hampering friendly force operations. In doing so, air, ground, and naval forces gain freedom of action and maneuver.[22] Bombers, through counter air operations can destroy enemy air forces on the ground, deny him the use of his own airfields, and destroy or cripple his ground-based air defenses and C^2 architecture. This competency requires bombers that possess superior targeting capability and a wide array of weapons to achieve the desired operational effect against an assortment of targets.

Global Attack entails the ability to strike anywhere on the globe at any time and encompasses both conventional and nuclear strike capability. Nuclear bomber capability must be maintained to deter the possibility of attack by rogue states. Likewise, nuclear-capable bombers provide a hedge against the proliferation of nuclear weapons throughout the world. Although current nuclear arsenals are certainly sufficient in number, the bomber force must continue to evolve in terms of strategy and C^2 architecture to remain a credible deterrent. From the standpoint of conventional operations, bombers will become the weapon of choice for crisis response and power projection just as they did during *Desert Strike*. This fact demands that bombers develop supportable C^2 systems and the capability to in-flight retarget any munition they employ.[23]

Similarly, bombers must become more effective in the competency of Rapid Global Mobility. This competency is crucial since it serves as the foundation for global power. Bomber forces must improve their ability to respond quickly and decisively from a deployed location. With US forces withdrawn from overseas bases, the demand for airlift during crisis responses will be staggering. In order to deploy rapidly and efficiently bombers must judiciously trim the size of their support packages and become effective partners in the Air Expeditionary Force (AEF) concept.[24]

Global Engagement's definition of Precision Engagement flows directly from the same concept found in *JV 2010*. Precision Engagement is the ability to apply precise force in order to achieve discriminate effects. Bombers require several capabilities to realize this core competency. The first is the information architecture to support dynamic battlefield management and target location functions. Second is the capability to accurately target and, if necessary, retarget weapons. Part and parcel of this ability is a supporting communications infrastructure capable of quickly, accurately, and securely transmitting and relaying huge volumes of digitized information. Bombers must also have the on-board capability of receiving, displaying, and manipulating targeting information, imagery, weather, and threat data. From a munitions standpoint, bombers must have a variety of flexible munitions including both unguided general purpose and accurate guided munitions. This competency and its supporting requirements will likely be the top priority for bombers for some time to come.[25]

Information Superiority and Agile Combat Support are both enablers of the bomber force. Information Superiority is absolutely crucial in the process of identifying, fixing, and targeting vital elements of enemy power. Similarly, accurate and timely target, threat, and force disposition information is essential to battle management and building aircrew situational awareness. In terms of sustainability, Agile Combat Support provides the wherewithal to generate combat sorties and maintain the required operations tempo. As operations tempos increase under parallel attack scenarios, bombers must streamline their logistics infrastructure and achieve better efficiencies in logistics practices in order to "stay in the game."[26]

Summary of Future Requirements

By examining the most pertinent studies and vision documents we can summarize future bomber requirements in the following table.

Table 4. Summation of Future Requirements

Source	Mission	Requirement			
		Avionics	Weaponry	Logistics	Training
2025 Gulliver's Travails	All	Precision targeting		Deploy rapidly Small footprint	Operate in NBC environments
Zaibatsu	All	Secure comm and data capability			
Digital Cacophony	All	Secure comm and data capability	Flexible munitions	Highly mobile	Operate under WMD attack Versatile operations
King Khan	All				Coalition ops MOOTW
Crossroads 2015	All	High tech comm and data systems Precision targeting		Deploy rapidly Highly mobile Sustained ops High ops tempo Prepositioned equipment Small footprint	Flexible ops

Source	Mission	Requirement			
		Avionics	Weaponry	Logistics	Training
Future War Peer Competitor	Strategic attack Interdiction	Data link Info processing	Flexible munitions	Small deployed support packages	Ops in corrupt information environments

43

		Secure comms Phased array radar w/MTI	Non-lethal weapons Brilliant munitions Advanced cruise missiles Advanced cluster bombs		Integration of on- and off-board sensors Long duration sorties Mission retasking
Niche Competitor	Strategic attack Interdiction	Data link Data processing Secure, high volume comms	Precision munitions GP weapons Brilliant munitions Large inventories		Joint operations Integration with ground offensive
JV2010	All	Data link Info processing Precision targeting Secure comm. On- and off-board strike assessment Self-protection	Precision munitions Advanced weapons	Rapid deployment Sustained ops High ops tempo Small support packages More efficient practices	Joint ops Coalition ops Long range ops Package ops
Global Engagement	All	Precision targeting Data link Secure C^2 comm. In-flight retargeting Info processing	GP weapons Guided munitions	Rapid deployment Small support packages Streamlined infrastructure More efficient practices	

Notes

[1] Air University, *Alternate Futures for 2025: Security Planning to Avoid Surprise* (Maxwell Air Force Base: Air University Press, September 1996), 1-17.

Notes

[2] *Alternate Futures for 2025*, 21-28.

[3] *Alternate Futures for 2025*, 29-35.

[4] *Alternate Futures for 2025*, 43-50.

[5] *Alternate Futures for 2025*, 51-52.

[6] *Alternate Futures for 2025*, 59-65.

[7] *Alternate Futures for 2025*, 66-71.

[8] *Alternate Futures for 2025*, 79-89.

[9] *Alternate Futures for 2025*, 107-113.

[10] *Alternate Futures for 2025*, 116.

[11] Jeffrey R. Barnett, *Future War: An Assessment of Aerospace Campaigns in 2010* (Maxwell Air Force Base: Air University Press, January 1996), xvii-xix.

[12] Barnett, 35-36.

[13] Barnett, 47-63.

[14] Barnett, 80-81.

[15] Barnett, 81-102.

[16] *Joint Vision 2010* (The Pentagon, Washington, D.C.: Office of the Chairman, Joint Chiefs of Staff, 1996), 1.

[17] *Joint Vision 2010*, 3-13.

[18] *Joint Vision 2010*, 20.

[19] *Joint Vision 2010*, 21.

[20] *Joint Vision 2010*, 24.

[21] *Global Engagement: A Vision for the 21st Century Air Force* (The Pentagon, Washington, D.C.: Department of the Air Force, 1996), 1-8.

[22] *Global Engagement*, 10.

[23] *Global Engagement*, 11.

[24] *Global Engagement*, 12.

[25] *Global Engagement*, 13.

[26] *Global Engagement*, 15-17.

Chapter 6

Synthesis of Requirements

Those who plan, program, and drive to an absolutely precise future will be precisely wrong. We must, in fact, approach the future through alternatives and understand what we can do to handle them.

--Gen Ronald R. Fogleman

General Fogleman's quote speaks volumes as to what's required of our bomber forces in the coming century. However, we are grossly unprepared for effective future bomber operations. Making matters worse, bomber modernization plans and operations concepts lack the vision to carry the force into the future.

The Air Force Bomber Roadmap establishes the concept of using bombers to provide initial attacks and sustained firepower for major regional conflicts. In support of this concept, it lays out a bomber modernization plan to upgrade bomber conventional capabilities. Its major flaw is that it addresses modernization only in terms of weapons while neglecting avionics upgrades and improved support concepts.[1] In fairness, the bomber requirements process subsequently addressed some of these additional issues, but even so, planned bomber upgrades fail to address the majority of the broad requirements we've gleaned from sources examined in this study. For example, funded B-1 modifications through fiscal year 2000 (FY2000) entail sorely needed aircraft and defensive system upgrades to bring the aircraft up to a suitable conventional configuration. Funded modifications also include Global Positioning System (GPS), JDAM, and WCMD integration, but the advanced thinking stops there. These upgrades are a far cry from the advanced technologies we should pursue for the "backbone of our nation's bomber force." The B-2 picture is somewhat better, but again funded upgrades are mainly those required to bring the aircraft up to its Block 30 configuration. By far the worst upgrade plan belongs to the B-52. Receiving only six percent of the bomber research and development budget, B-52 upgrades are limited mainly to reliability and maintainability items. Although the B-52 currently enjoys the greatest flexibility and conventional capability in the bomber force, this modernization plan doesn't bode well for an aircraft that's programmed for service until the year 2030.

Likewise, the bomber concept of operations is in serious jeopardy. The Air Force may ultimately be unable to implement this ConOps since its success hinges on completing the modernization programs contained in the Bomber Roadmap. In fact, the current program of upgrades isn't even scheduled for completion until 2006. In addition, the Air Force has been unable to achieve and maintain acceptable mission capable rates and sustain deployed operations with the B-1 and B-2.[2] For weapons systems that are the leading edge of US long-range power projection capability, we've apparently neglected their well-being and are guilty of myopic vision despite our rhetoric. Even worse are the sins of the bomber community against itself.

Air Force leadership, and bomber leadership in particular, has failed to keep pace with changing times. The advent of ACC should have been a signal to change mindsets in both the fighter and heavy communities, however, both factions are stuck in a rut. We've not yet evolved to the concept of a strike team and for the most part remain worlds apart in training philosophies. For example, bomber training has remained stilted in a SIOP mindset. To this day, bomb wing "live drop" sorties on weapons ranges remain few and far between. Even more scarce are training sorties which integrate bombers into force packages. Other than occasional trips to Red Flag, bomb wings shy away from participation in joint and composite training. Maintainers and logisticians in the bomber community are just as guilty of stagnation. It's a rare day when munitions assembly and load teams get to prepare a full-up weapons load for actual release. Rarer still is the opportunity to participate in deployed operations. Even then, bomber maintainers don't get to experience the stress of high operations tempos as bomb wing deployment packages are typically bloated with as many as 200 technicians to maintain as few as four deployed aircraft. The bomber community simply has to think more realistically in terms of training and logistics if it wants to compete as a viable combat force in future conflict.

Our efforts to precisely nail down bomber requirements in light of future conflict can be summed up in one phrase, "maximize flexibility." Our world is too uncertain to determine which paths will lead to specific alternate future. Furthermore, betting incorrectly on one of these futures has drastic consequences. Nothing could be worse than acquiring systems that are completely ill-suited for future conflict. Therefore, remaining flexible in our approach to bomber requirements isn't such bad advice.

Looking at bomber operations from a historical perspective proves this point. Traditional bomber missions have remained intact since WWII meaning that some requirements are enduring. Examples include the need for long range, large payloads, specialized weaponry, and training in force package integration. But, despite traditional thinking on applications of bomber aircraft, evolutions in the nature of various conflicts led to improvisation in the use of bombers. Even though the primary emphasis may have remained on traditional missions, bombers were pressed into a wide array of roles ranging from strategic attack to CAS, and even defense suppression. These unique roles demonstrated the need for items such as adaptable munitions, broad communications capability, night operations, and specialized targeting capability. From a more current standpoint, references ranging from our National Security Strategy to Air Force Doctrine demand even more out of our bomber force structure than traditional missions, while studies of future conflict demand a quantum leap in those requirements.

As displayed in the summary tables at the end of the historical, current, and future perspective chapters, we can broadly state these requirements in terms of avionics, weaponry, logistics, and training. And for purposes of implementation, we can address requirements in terms of immediate actions and what must be done down the road (2005-2010 timeframe) in order to equip ourselves for conflict in 2015 and beyond.

Immediate Actions

Avionics

Achieve military standard (MIL STD) 1760 Data Bus integration on all three bombers – this modification enables aircraft to carry the new advanced munitions utilizing inertial navigation system (INS) and/or GPS guidance. This equipment enables the aircraft to put a present position into the weapon before release so that it can navigate and guide to the proper target coordinates. Currently, the B-1 has no 1760 capability, the B-2 has it only on its rotary launcher assembly, and the B-52 has 1760 only on external stations. 1760 integration will enhance compatibility with JDAM, JSOW, JASSM, and WCMD facilitating attacks on a wide variety of target sets.

Pursue Link 16 and Joint Tactical Information Distribution System (JTIDS) integration for all three bombers – these systems meet the requirements for common data link capability and aid in both retargeting of enroute strike sorties and establishing aircrew situational awareness. Capabilities include near real-time tactical information; up-to-the-minute battlefield information from thousands of US and allied participants; and the ability to exchange secure, jam-resistant target, threat, and navigation information on a reliable, interoperable basis.

Pursue beyond-line-of-sight (BLOS) voice and data capability and HAVE QUICK II integration on all three bombers – this modification provides satellite communication using demand assignment multiple access for LOS and BLOS voice and data transmissions. It permits near global, highly reliable, point-to-point transmission capability enhancing C^2 during power projection missions. It also provides reliable BLOS communication with AWACS, JSTARs, ABCCC, RIVET JOINT aircraft, and major Air Force ground nodes. HAVE QUICK II provides jam resistant communications within LOS of all friendly aircraft and ground nodes. Currently, only the B-2 lacks this capability.

Weaponry

Expand weapons integration of JDAM, JSOW, JASSM, and WCMD to all three bombers – in conjunction with MIL STD 1760 integration, this action allows all three bombers to employ the same weapons against a wide variety of targets and avoids the burden of weapons specialization on the logistics and supply system. These weapons will

50

also be common to fighter aircraft simplifying the weapons allocation process within theaters.

Logistics

Pursue a common bomb rack system compatible with all three bombers – this system must also have provisions for 1760 data bus interface. A common internal carriage assembly simplifies the basing of all three bombers together at common forward operating locations, eases the burden on the logistics pipeline, and provides better maintainability and reliability. Likewise, it streamlines munitions upload contributing to faster turn times and higher sortie production.

Obtain 30-day Mission Readiness Spares Packages (MRSP) for all three bombers – MRSPs provide spare parts for deployed operations and allow a weapons system to conduct operations without resupply for a specified time period. After this period, the deployed location must tap into an existing logistics pipeline to continue operations. Currently, only the B-52 is funded for 30-day packages; the other two bombers only have 14-day packages. By expanding all packages to 30 days, bombers will be able to sustain higher operations tempos for longer periods of time before resupply becomes necessary.

Conduct reviews utilizing "outside expertise" of all bomber main and deployed operating base maintenance practices – these audits must focus on identifying prudent reductions in pre-, post-, and thru-flight maintenance actions. Likewise, the review should encompass all backshop as well as sortie generation practices. Practices such as "hot pit" refueling and concurrent arming/fueling should be explored. The goal of these reductions is to increase aircraft availability and sortie generation rates.

Reduce the size of bomber deployment packages to a minimum – review MRSP contents to validate spares quantities. Review required specialty skills with emphasis on reducing required manpower by cross-utilizing specialties during deployed operations.

Training

Review conventional and nuclear flying training unit (FTU) syllabi for all three bombers – this review should focus on providing effective and appropriate training for future combat crews. More emphasis must be placed on utilizing new computerized mission planning systems, weapons training, threat knowledge, developing tactical awareness, night operations, and formation operations.

Review all bomber unit training programs – ensure that all unit training programs build on the foundation provided by FTU programs. Likewise, ensure that all units train to employ the actual weapons and delivery tactics required by unit designed operational capability (DOC) statements and theater operations plans against which units are tasked. In addition, all unit crewmembers should receive flight and academic training emphasizing integration into joint and combined operations. Moreover, all unit training programs must emphasize operations flexibility – crews must be prepared to operate in environments contaminated by NBC agents and corrupt information. Additionally, crews should routinely participate in training sorties and exercises where both formations and single aircraft are retasked against alternate targets or tasked to restrike a specific target within a range complex. This training must encompass all direct attack and guided weapons employed by the unit.

Train bomber aircrews to integrate with, and utilize targeting data available from third-party assets such as JSTARs, P-3, and S-3 platforms – properly training aircrews to integrate with these platforms eliminates the present shortcomings in resolution of on-board targeting systems. Developing this capability increases the ability of bombers to engage ground forces on the move as well as theater ballistic missiles during pre-launch phases.

Long-Term Actions

Avionics

Pursue phased array ground mapping radars with moving target indicator (MTI) capability for all three bombers – this upgrade provides the ability to locate, track, and target advancing ground forces. Phased array radar also facilitates the ability to perform differential GPS targeting enhancing the accuracy of GPS-guided weapons. In addition, phased array radars are more reliable which increases mean time between failure, reduces maintenance requirements, and reduces requirements for replacement parts. If possible, this radar should be common to all three aircraft. This will give each bomber the ability to independently target, strike, and reattack advancing armored columns. Currently, only the B-2 has limited capability in this area.

Develop simplified aircraft weapons management computer architectures – these computer architectures should focus on rapid weapons selection, targeting, and retargeting routines. The processes should utilize "windows" formats with all weapons data contained in easily accessible "pull-down" menus. The same basic format should be utilized for all weapons certified on the aircraft.

Develop new suites of bomber on-board sensors to aid in navigation and targeting – these suites should include a robust array of both passive and active sensors including radar, infrared, and low-light optics. These sensors must encompass a wide range of frequencies allowing comparative "looks" at terrain features and targets to ensure accuracy and eliminate electronic and visual "spoofing" by the enemy. This effort directly enhances our ability to fix, track, and engage vital targets.

Develop bomber communications suites and on-board processors capable of transmitting, receiving, and manipulating data resulting from the fusion of intelligence assets and advances in C^2 architecture – these systems must be capable of receiving and transmitting data in the same form utilized by friendly intelligence networks. These systems must be fast, secure, jam-proof, and easily operated by the aircrew. Likewise, on-board processors must be able to manipulate and display data in a variety of forms (threat data, targeting information, message traffic, weather data, and digital imagery). These systems contribute to establishing effective long-range C^2, battlefield awareness, and rapid retargeting of strike sorties.

Weaponry

Develop medium-range stand-off weapons capable of precision accuracy without the aid of GPS or other forms of off-board navigation inputs – weapons of this type will maintain desired levels of accuracy and eliminate the possibility of enemy denial of navigation signals.

Develop cruise missiles incorporating extended range, precision accuracy, a variety of warheads, advanced stealth technology, and navigation routines that don't rely on external inputs – cruise missiles utilizing these technologies will increase survivability and increase our capability to strike anything from area targets to buried/hardened targets. They also eliminate the threat of navigation signal denial, reduce the possibility of missile intercept, and provide greater flexibility to retarget missiles enroute to the launch point.

Develop new families of low cost general purpose and canister weapons emphasizing high-yield explosives and anti-armor/personnel capabilities – these weapons will increase bomber capabilities to efficiently cover area targets while keeping per-unit weapons costs as low as possible.

Develop weapons fuzes with a wide range of cockpit selectable settings adaptable to a large array of weapons – this effort should encompass both height measuring and timed fuzes allowing the crew to determine the optimum fuze setting based on the weapon carried and the tasked target. The fuze setting must be cockpit selectable in order to enhance the flexibility of bombers in a retargeting scenario. These fuzes must be adaptable to general purpose as well as guided weapons. Fuzes of this type would allow a crew to attack anything from surface targets to hardened structures with the same weapons load.

Logistics

Develop an information architecture to support lean deployments and "just-in-time" resupply efforts – when resupply is immediately available, this advanced information architecture will allow the downsizing of spares packages initially deployed with units. As resupply efforts commence, accurate information on spares requirements will minimize the impact on available lift by ensuring the right parts and consumables arrive in the correct quantities at the correct destinations as needed.

Develop new methods of packaging and handling MRSP contents – take advantage of advanced, lightweight packaging materials and containers. This initiative drives required deployment volumes to absolute minimums in order to reduce lift requirements.

Expand use of prepositioned materials – preposition as much support equipment and weaponry as feasible to reduce lift requirements.

Develop low-cost and expeditious methods of detecting and repairing flaws on low-observable surfaces – this initiative is applicable to both aircraft and weapons. It entails development of compact, low cost diagnostic tools and quick, efficient methods of repairing surface treatments. These actions hold weapon system life cycle costs to a minimum and maximize system availability to enhance operations tempo.

Training

Conduct periodic reviews of unit training programs to ensure training keeps pace with new weapons, employment concepts, and potential theater taskings – training should be stressful enough to determine weaknesses.

Enhance simulator capabilities to offer the highest fidelity levels possible in terms of employment training – this effort entails keeping simulator visuals, threat libraries, and weapons data up-to-date. In addition, simulators must be capable of training employment scenarios such as off-board targeting, retargeting, and package integration. On-line training with other units and platforms should be integrated as well.

Notes

[1] *The Bomber Roadmap: Enhancing the Nation's Conventional Bomber Force* (Washington, D.C.: The Department of the Air Force, Jan. 1995).

[2] *Air Force Bombers – Options to Retire or Restructure the Force Would Reduce Planned Spending*, GAO Report NSIAD-96-192 (Washington D.C.: The Government Accounting Office, September 1996), 3.0.

Chapter 7

Conclusions

These immediate and long-term actions are but a sample of capabilities required in our bomber force. Items like these flow directly from requirements generated by the methodology in this study.

We began this study by determining if the nation even requires a bomber force in the future. Based on the leverage provided by bombers in terms of mass and firepower, they are certainly flexible and efficient weapons systems. Likewise, in the nuclear arena they provide a very visible and potent deterrent to aggression. But more importantly, in a future of shrinking force structure and reduced overseas presence, the bomber may provide the only means of striking in distant theaters as we begin deploying other forces. Bombers provide the crucial ability to fight while others deploy.

With this issue resolved, we traced the history of bomber roles in selected air battles since WWII and then moved on to an examination of bomber requirements in terms of current and future conflict. One common thread revealed by examining bomber operations in a historical context is that flexibility is the key to successful bomber employment. The classic bomber missions of strategic attack and interdiction remained consistent, however, the methods of employing bombers varied dramatically. Night operations, package integration, off-board targeting, and even the flexibility to engage in new roles like CAS, contributed to the effective employment of bombers and attaining the objectives of the theater commander. The same common threads are present in current concepts of warfare.

In documents ranging from our National Security Strategy through Air Force basic doctrine, the key to successful air combat is flexibility in all operations. US forces must be capable of engaging across the entire conflict spectrum, either independently or as part of the joint team. Forces must also be capable of operating in information corrupt and NBC contaminated environments. Rapid mobility and high operations tempos are consistent themes. These qualities are placed at an even higher premium in terms of future conflict.

Future studies like *Alternate Futures for 2025* and *Future War* point to the evolving environment of warfare. Bolstered by vision pieces such as *JV2010* and *Global Engagement*, it's apparent that these qualities become even more important after the turn of the century. Rapid mobility, sustainment, and high ops tempos are absolutely essential to prevail in future conflict. The ability to precisely engage a world-wide array of time-critical targets while underpinned by an information architecture providing dominant battlespace awareness is paramount. Although the basic mission for bombers will likely remain unchanged, the pace of operations will certainly accelerate. This rapid pace of operations, coupled with long bomber flight times from the CONUS or deployed locations leads us to the key requirement of flexibility. Our bomber force is not currently well-suited to these types of operations.

Our current bomber capabilities will not meet the requirements of future conflicts. Our training programs and logistics practices can't keep pace in this dynamic environment. The bomber community is stuck in the SIOP mold of fixed targets, long planning cycles, and employment training that lacks imagination and flexibility. Not far behind in obsolescence are our weapons and avionics systems. Bomber modernization programs are attempting to rectify weapons shortfalls, but this is occurring at the expense of every other facet of our mission. Although we've been able to muddle through in recent operations like *Desert Strike*, the pace of future operations will leave bomber forces wanting for new capability unless we begin to take action now.

With the nature of future conflict pointing to the fact that bombers may indeed be the weapon of choice, our modernization effort must expand to address other requirements. As I've shown by examining the historical, current, and future contexts of bomber operations, these requirements fall into four categories: avionics, weaponry, logistics, and training. Only by addressing these areas can we hope to compete and remain an effective tool for supporting national objectives. I've offered a few points of departure for a comprehensive bomber modernization effort, but this is certainly not the end. Air Force and bomber leadership must keep an open mind and one eye on the future to ensure that our bomber force keeps pace with the evolving nature of conflict. If we fail, the bomber detractors will rightfully win, but the nation will lose. We can't afford to relegate these national assets to the tar pit.

Glossary

AB	Air Base
ABCCC	Airborne Battlefield Command and Control Center
ACC	Air Combat Command
AEF	Air Expeditionary Force
AF	Air Force
AFB	Air Force Base
AFDD	Air Force Doctrine Document
AGM	air-to-ground missile
AOR	area of responsibility
ATO	air tasking order
AWACS	Airborne Warning and Control System
BLOS	beyond line-of-sight
C^2	command and control
CAS	close air support
CBU	cluster bomb unit
CENTCOM	US Central Command
CINC	commander in chief of a combatant command
CINCCENT	Commander-in-Chief, US Central Command
CONOPS	concept of operations
CONUS	continental United States
DMPI	desired mean point of impact
DOC	designed operational capability
DMZ	demilitarized zone
ECM	electronic countermeasures (now termed electronic protect)
ELINT	electronic intelligence
FTU	flying training unit
FY	fiscal year
GBU	guided bomb unit
GP	general purpose
GPS	Global Positioning System

ICBM	intercontinental ballistic missile
INS	inertial navigation system
ISR	intelligence, surveillance, and reconnaissance
JASSM	Joint Air-to-Surface Stand-off Missile
JCS	Joint Chiefs of Staff
JDAM	Joint Direct Attack Munition
JFACC	joint force air component commander
JFC	joint force commander
JFICC	joint force information component commander
JSOW	Joint Stand-off Weapon
JSTARS	Joint Surveillance Target Attack Radar System
JTIDS	Joint Tactical Information Distribution System
JV 2010	*Joint Vision 2010*
LOC	lines of communication
LOS	line-of-sight
MAA	mission area assessment
MAD	mutual assured destruction
MAJCOM	major command
MAT	mission area team
MIL STD	military standard
Mk	mark (weapon version designator)
MNA	mission needs analysis
MOOTW	military operations other than war
MPABA	Malayan Peoples' Anti-British Army
MPP	modernization planning process
MRSP	mission readiness spares package
MSA	mission solution analysis
MTI	moving target indicator
NAF	numbered air force
NBC	nuclear, biological, and chemical
NCA	national command authorities
NMS	National Military Strategy
NSS	National Security Strategy
NVA	North Vietnamese Army
NVN	North Vietnam
PGM	precision guided munition
pub	publication
SAC	Strategic Air Command
SAM	surface-to-air missile

SEAD	suppression of enemy air defenses
SIGINT	signals intelligence
SIOP	single integrated operations plan
SOF	special operations forces
UN	United Nations
US	United States
USAF	United States Air Force
WCMD	Wind Corrected Munitions Dispenser
WMD	weapons of mass destruction
WWII	World War II

air and space power. The synergistic application of air space, and information systems to project global strategic military power.

air campaign. A connected series of operations conducted by air forces to achieve joint force objectives within a given time and area.

air interdiction. Air operations conducted to destroy, neutralize, or delay the enemy's military potential before it can be brought to bear effectively against friendly forces at such distance from friendly forces that detailed integration of each air mission with the fire and movement of friendly forces is not required.

airlift. Operations to transport and deliver forces and materiel through the air in support of strategic, operational, and tactical objectives.

air refueling. The capability to refuel aircraft in flight, which extends presence, increases range, and allows air forces to bypass areas of potential trouble.

air superiority. That degree of dominance in the air battle of one force over another which permits the conduct of operations by the former and its related land, sea, and air forces at a given time and place without prohibitive interference by the opposing force.

air tasking order. A method used to task and disseminate to components, subordinate units, and command and control agencies those projected sorties/capabilities/forces to targets and specific missions. Normally provides specific instructions to include call signs, targets, controlling agencies, etc., as well as general instructions. Also called ATO.

campaign. A series of related military operations aimed at accomplishing a strategic or operational objective within a given space and time.

campaign plan. A plan for a series of related military operations aimed to achieve strategic and operational objectives within a given time and space.

centers of gravity. Those characteristics, capabilities, or localities from which a military force derives its freedom of action, physical strength, or will to fight.

close air support. Air action by fixed- and rotary-wing aircraft against hostile targets which are in close proximity to friendly forces and which require detailed integration of each air mission with the fire and movement of those forces. Also called CAS.

coalition. An ad hoc arrangement between two or more nations for common action.

coalition force. A force composed of military elements of nations that have formed a temporary alliance for some specific purpose.

combat search and rescue. A specific task performed by rescue forces to effect the recovery of distressed personnel during war or military operations other than war. Also called CSAR.

command and control. The exercise of authority and direction by a properly designated commander over assigned and attached forces in the accomplishment of the mission. Command and control functions are performed through an arrangement of personnel, equipment, communications, facilities, and procedures employed by a commander in planning, directing, coordinating, and controlling forces and operations in accomplishment of the mission. Also called C^2.

concept of operations. A verbal or graphic statement, in broad outline, of a commander's assumptions or intent in regard to an operation or series of operations. The concept of operations frequently is embodied in campaign plans and operation plans; in the latter case, particularly when the plans cover a series of connected operations to be carried out simultaneously or in succession. The concept is designed to give an overall picture of the operation. It is included primarily for additional clarity of purpose. Also called commander's concept.

core competency. The basic areas of expertise or the specialties that the Air Force brings to any activity across the spectrum of military operations whether as a single Service or in conjunction with the core competencies of other Services in joint operations. Core competencies represent both air and space power application theory and physical capability represented in a well-trained and equipped air force.

counterair. A US Air Force term for air operations conducted to attain and maintain a desired degree of air superiority by the destruction or neutralization of enemy forces. Both air offensive and air defensive actions are involved. The former range throughout enemy territory and are generally conducted at the initiative of the friendly forces. The latter are conducted near or over friendly territory and are generally reactive to the initiative of the enemy air forces.

employment. The strategic, operational, and tactical use of forces.

expeditionary force. An armed force organized to accomplish a specific objective in a foreign country.

information warfare. Actions taken to achieve information superiority by affecting adversary information, information-based processes, and information systems, while defending one's own information, information-based processes, and information systems.

joint force. A general term applied to a force composed of significant elements, assigned or attached, of two or more Military Departments, operating under a single joint force commander.

joint operations. A general term to describe military actions conducted by joint forces, or by Service forces in relationships (e.g., support, coordinating authority), which, of themselves, do not create joint forces.

mobility. A quality or capability of military forces which permits them to move from place to place while retaining the ability to fulfill their primary mission.

national military strategy. The art and science of distributing and applying military power to attain national objectives in peace and war.

national security strategy. The art and science of developing, applying, and coordinating the instruments of national power (diplomatic, economic, military, and informational) to achieve objectives that contribute to national security. Also called national strategy or grand strategy.

reconnaissance. A mission undertaken to obtain, by visual observation or other detection methods, information about the activities and resources of an enemy or potential enemy; or to secure data concerning the meteorological, hydrographic, or geographic characteristics of a particular area.

sortie. In air operation, an operational flight by one aircraft.

strategic mission. A mission directed against one or more of a selected series of enemy targets with the purpose of progressive destruction and disintegration of the enemy's warmaking capacity and his will to make war. Targets include key manufacturing systems, sources or raw material, critical material, stockpiles, power systems, transportation systems, communications facilities, and other such target systems. As opposed to tactical operations, strategic operations are designed to have a long-range, rather than immediate, effect on the enemy and its military forces.

strike. An attack which is intended to inflict damage on, seize, or destroy an objective.

surveillance. The systematic observation of aerospace, surface or subsurface areas, places, persons, or things, by visual, aural, electronic, photographic, or other means.

targeting. 1. The process of selecting targets and matching the appropriate response to them, taking account of operational requirements and capabilities. 2. The analysis of enemy situations relative to the commander's mission, objectives, and capabilities at the commander's disposal, to identify and nominate specific vulnerabilities that, if exploited, will accomplish the commander's purpose through delaying, disrupting, disabling, or destroying enemy forces or resources critical to the enemy.

target system. 1. All the targets situated in a particular geographic area and functionally related. 2. A group of targets which are so related that their destruction will produce some particular effect desired by the attacker.

Bibliography

"Air Force Doctrine Document 1: Air Force Basic Doctrine." Maxwell Air Force Base AL: Headquarters Air Force Doctrine Center, September 1997.

Air University, *Alternate Futures for 2025: Security Planning to Avoid Surprise.* Maxwell Air Force Base AL: Air University Press, September 1996.

Barnett, Jeffrey R., Colonel, USAF. *Future War: An Assessment of Aerospace Campaigns in 2010.* Maxwell Air Force Base AL: Air University Press, January 1996.

"The Bomber Roadmap: Enhancing the Nation's Conventional Bomber Force." Washington, D.C.: The Department of the Air Force, January 1995.

Briefing. Headquarters Air Combat Command Director of Requirements. Subject: Air Combat Command Modernization Planning Process. Langley Air Force Base VA, 1997.

Clodfelter, Mark, *The Limits of Airpower: The American Bombing of North Vietnam.* New York: The Free Press, 1989.

Eschmann, Karl J., *LINEBACKER: The Untold Story of the Air Raids Over North Vietnam.* New York: Ballantine Books, 1989.

Flintham, Victor, *Air Wars and Aircraft: A Detailed Record of Air Combat, 1945 to the Present.* New York: Facts on File, 1990.

Fogleman, Ronald R., General, Chief of Staff, USAF. "The Contribution of Bombers to America's Deep Strike Capability" Address. The Toqueville Group, Capitol Hill, Washington, D.C., 13 September 1996.

Futrell, Robert F., *The United States Air Force in Korea, 1950-1953.* Washington, D.C.: Office of Air Force History, 1983.

"Global Engagement: A Vision for the 21st Century Air Force." Washington, D.C.: The Department of the Air Force, The Pentagon, 1996.

Government Accounting Office. "Report #NSIAD-96-192: Air Force Bombers – Options to Retire or Restructure the Force Would Reduce Planned Spending." Washington, D.C., September 1996.

"Gulf War Air Power Survey, Volume II, Part I, Operations." Washington, D.C.: Government Printing Office, 1993.

"Gulf War Air Power Survey, Volume II, Part II, Effects and Effectiveness." Washington, D.C.: Government Printing Office, 1993.

Hallion, Richard P., *Storm Over Iraq: Air Power and the Gulf War.* Washington, D.C.: Smithsonian Institution Press, 1992.

The Joint Chiefs of Staff. "Joint Pub 1: Joint Warfare of the Armed Forces of the United States." Washington, D.C.: Government Printing Office, 10 January 1995.

The Joint Chiefs of Staff. "Joint Pub 3-0: Doctrine for Joint Operations." Washington, D.C.: Government Printing Office, 1 February 1995.

Momyer, William W., General, USAF (Ret), *Air Power in Three Wars*. Washington, D.C.: US Government Printing Office, 1978.

"National Military Strategy: Shape, Respond, Prepare Now – A Military Strategy for a New Era." Washington, D.C.: Joint Chiefs of Staff, 1997). On-line, Defense Technical Information Center, World Wide Web, 16 December 1997.

President of the United States. "A National Security Strategy for a New Century." Washington, D.C.: The White House, 1997.

Shalikashvili, John M., General, USA, Chairman of the Joint Chiefs of Staff. "Joint Vision 2010." Washington, D.C.: Office of the Chairman of the Joint Chiefs of Staff, July 1996.

Somerville, Terry, "B-52s Lead Attack on Iraq." Air Force News Service, 5 September 1996.

Tilford, Earl H. Jr., *Setup: What the Air Force Did in Vietnam and Why*. Maxwell Air Force Base AL: Air University Press, 1991.

White Paper. Strategic Aerospace Warfare Study Panel. "Aerospace Power for the 21st Century: A Theory to Fly By." Maxwell Air Force Base AL, 1996.

Winnefeld, James A., Preston Niblack, and Dana J. Johnson, *A League of Airmen: US Air Power in the Gulf War*. Santa Monica CA: RAND Project Air Force, 1994.

DISTRIBUTION A:

Approved for public release; distribution is unlimited.

Air War College
Maxwell AFB, Al 36112